JOURNEY TO PLANET POSITIVE

Inspirational Poetry and Thoughts

Linda L Andrusko

Enjoy!
Linda Andrusko

© 2012 by the author of this book. The book author retains sole copyright to her contributions to this book.

All rights reserved. No part of this book may be reproduced, stored in a retrieval system or transmitted in any form or by any means without the prior written permission of the author.

In loving memory of Earl and Frances

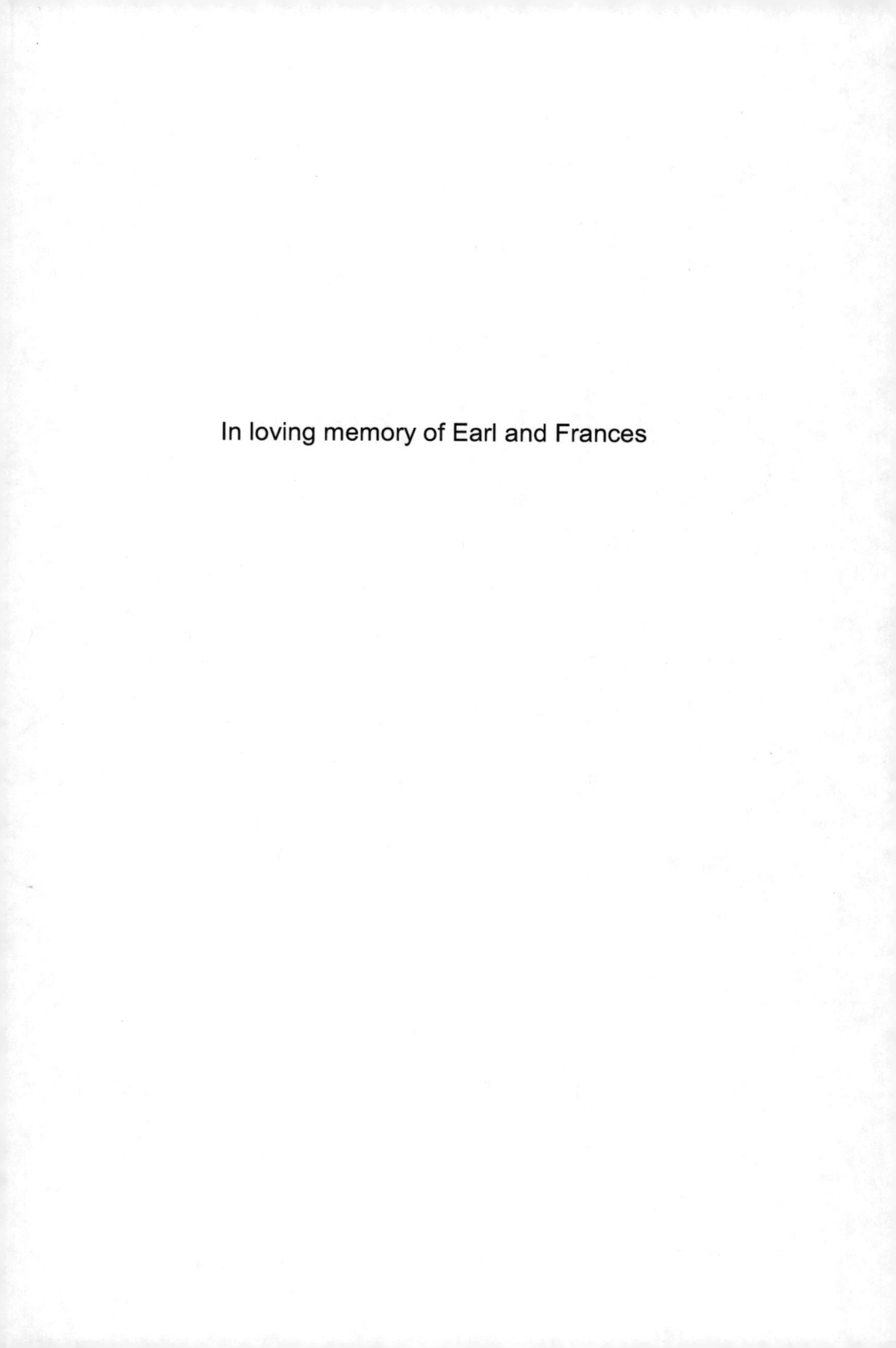

Table of Contents

Nature and Places

Seasons Flying By
By the Pier
First of Spring
Serenity at Lake Crescent
Emergence of Autumn
Black Tailed Deer
Standing Solitary
A Day with the Dolphins
Fire and Ice
Seeds of Life
Love of Nature
Snowflake
Prisms of Light
Rainbows and Moonbeams
Surrendered Thoughts
Oceans of Life
Sands of Time
Visions of Pacific Northwest
Flight of Fantasy
The Blue Hole
Reflections of Light
Bounty of Autumn
Spring a New Beginning
Sunrise
Sunset
Called to Hurricane Ridge

Musically Inspired

He Awaits the Muse
Snowfall on Saint James
Dance of Passion
Life's Musical Notes
Connections
First of August
Soothing Music

Music's Feeling
The Greatest Things
Intensity
Rekindling of Passion
Into the Black
Seasons
Voyage

Honoring Our Military

Mission of Love
Commitment of Unconditional Love
Love Letters from Afar
Still the Same
Praying for Peace

Love and Romance

Children of Love
A Kiss at Sunrise
Expressions of Love
When Two Souls Join as One
Outpouring of Love
A Path with Heart
Empowered by Love
Motivated by Love
Message in a Bottle

Humor and Whimsy

Green Machine
Chicken Soup
Mile Wide Smile
Sticky Notes
Little Things
Magic Carpet Ride
Imagination

Uplifting Thoughts of Hope

Recipe for a Smile
In Your Direction
When You Believe
Road Leading to Love

Led by Spirit
Sunshine in Your Heart
Back to Center Core
Colors
Look Towards the Light
Giving Divine Direction
New Beginning
Colors of Pompoms
If I Were a Rainbow
Pretty Paper
The Source
Beacon of Light
Learning Curve
Perpetual Motion
Acceptance
Destiny of the Heart
Heightened Senses
Never Stop Dreaming
Blessings of Thanksgiving
Words You Utter
Depth Perception
Facing the Unknown
Believe
I Lifted My Eyes
Path without Fear
Jigsaw Puzzle
United We Stand
Seeing the Light
Look Towards Tomorrow
Escape from Negativity
When Life Gets Tough
I B M
Cheerful Heart
Miracles
Behold the Sunshine
Crossroads of Life
Into the Fold
Guiding Light
Into the Light
Love of Life

Acknowledgements

I give big thanks to my cousin, Shari for the idea and inspiration of "Planet Positive" used in my title.

I give thanks to Yanni for the inspiration to write through his book "Yanni in Words" as well as many members of his message board who encouraged me to continue writing.

Some of the writings are in support of our troops, in thankfulness for their courage to risk their lives to protect us, as well as promoting peace around the world for Mankind.

I thank my husband, George for his support while writing this book.

I must give love and thanks to my dear friend and sister in love and light, Dara Marie for her encouragement and moral support.

I am also thankful to my departed father, who told me that he felt I would be a good writer.

JOURNEY TO PLANET POSITIVE

Seasons Flying By

Faster and faster, the seasons go
Hot sun, rain and then snow
Appreciating each day at my pace
Seasons flying by like a race

Savoring every leaf and cloud
Will not get lost in the crowd
Smelling each flower that I see
Like a butterfly being set free

Precious life that goes too fast
Remembering those from my past
As the day merges into night
Watching birds taking flight

Sometimes aging is not so kind
Staying young still in my mind
Being grateful when I awake
Taking life for granted; a big mistake

I never know when life might end
Each breath I take is my friend
As I watch the squirrels scurry
I realize I must not hurry

Seasons will go by; this I know
On my face, a smile will show
If next winter seems too long
I will think about spring's sweet song

By the Pier

Standing quietly by the pier
Only subtle sounds do we hear
Sunset's red hues in the sky
A winter hawk is flying by

Gentle waves coming in to shore
We could not want any more
Deer walking at the water's edge
Up on a bluff, we stand at the ledge

Sun's reflections dancing on the ocean
We are filled with deep emotion
A gentle breeze against our faces
Observing one of God's special places

In the distance, a ship passes in the night
We watch until it is out of sight
Darkness comes, but then we know
Tomorrow by the pier, will be another show

First of Spring

First of spring, how my heart sings
Your season brings such sweet things
The thought of going outside
Driving along, taking a long ride

Watching the birds being born
Winter blues gone, no longer forlorn
Soon I see a beautiful butterfly
Such a sight makes me sigh

Feeling young and wanting to run
I feel the fresh air and warmth of the sun
No more dark clouds get in the way
Dancing in the meadow, music will play

First of spring brings new life
How can anyone feel any strife?
Seeing the first buds on the trees
Seeing the last of all deep freeze

Spring is my favorite, I have found
Nature's beauty is abound
For the moment I cannot wait
First of spring, do not be late

Serenity at Lake Crescent

Sun shines down upon shimmering water
A lake so quiet; no fish or otter
One could sit and write a psalm
Around your shores is peace and calm

Sunlight sparkled as if a wand
Sprinkled beams on 'golden pond'
At water's edge, there was no sound
Peacefulness is what we found

Surrounded by mountains, the lake below
Summoned to us; there we should go
Evergreen trees around each bend
The warm feeling could never end

A Heavenly reminder of what He gives
A confirmation that nature lives
Wonder and beauty is so grand
We will continue to protect this land

We looked at treetops laced with snow
Happiness in our hearts is what we know
As God continues to uplift
Serenity at Lake Crescent is His gift

Emergence of Autumn

As I look outside of my window, I see rain clouds in the sky, snow on the mountain tops, the hills still green but laced with colorful trees which are changing gradually. This is the first sign of autumn, as summer has quickly left us with cooler temperatures, less hours of sunlight, and the promise of a new season. At night the stars and moon shine brightly, after a glorious sunset, which appears different and more spectacular each time I see it happen.

With the emergence of autumn, another season holds the promise of new adventures, challenges, pondering of what life holds in store for each of us. It is exciting because we are offered another portion of time, with much to look forward to, not knowing what to expect. I look at the unknown as a fun adventure, and with a positive attitude. God gives us something new each and every day.

There is something new and glorious about each season, but autumn is one of my favorites, although one of the shortest seasons. I always look forward to taking rides to see the colors change; how the hills come alive with orange, yellow and rust colors, with the darkness of the mountains as a back drop, only starting to be capped with bright white snow. I could stare at that picture for hours, but revel in each moment of time given to me to enjoy this glorious show of nature, season after season. I can only pray that next year, I can watch this process happen again, as nothing is taken for granted, especially life on this beautiful earth.

God has painted a gigantic picture for us to behold, enjoy, see, touch and love. If only more people can take moments from their busy lives, stop fretting, complaining, hating, fearing, or feeling hopeless, they will be able to see the possibilities that God and nature has given them. More than ever, it is a time to relax and appreciate what we have, whether it be abundance or very little. Autumn is free to everyone, and guaranteed to be offered without our being asked for anything in return, other than to nurture and care for it, as well as for each other. Each time you look outside of your window, smile because what you see belongs to you and all of us.

Black Tailed Deer

On a bright spring day, we stood in a living room witnessing the prophecy happen, just as she told me it would.

Four young black tailed deer sauntered across the bottom of her deep back yard, just as quietly and serenely as could be. They stopped only to casually graze upon this seemingly sacred land, without any fear or worry about three humans who were watching them in awe behind the glass windows.

It is believed by Native people that the deer represents gentleness, compassion and kindness. There is no doubt of this as we watch them, as if our eyes were glued to their beauty and wonder.

One might ponder why it is that many human beings on our planet do not demonstrate what these fine animals teach us. How wonderful it would be, if every human being would act with these three attributes, treating each other with gentleness, compassion and kindness. What a wonderful world this would genuinely be.

I have loved deer since the first time I stared at a picture on my bedroom wall, at about the age of five. My mother told me a story about when she and my father, before I was born, went to a National Park in California. She was about five months along with me then. They sat down on a park bench to have some lunch, when a doe came out of the woods, walked over to my mother, and put her head right onto my mom's stomach. Then the doe tried to get into the car with my mother, when they went to leave. I have had a connection with deer all of my life, and finally got to hold one when I was in my thirties. Deer will always be my favorite animal, and I always stop, as if frozen in time when they appear.

As always, that day when those young black tailed deer walked by, it was a special and spiritual moment in time for all of us. I know that living in this land will bring more special times like that in the future, and we will hold these precious animals in high reverence, as God's special creatures on our Earth. We will be grateful forever, for Him sharing them during this time and space with us.

Standing Solitary

Standing at the water's edge, so quietly do the boats move to the morning's gentle waves. There is not a soul in sight; only the gradual lifting of the fog over the water. I can just begin to see the hills in the background, with their trees lifting towards a cloudy sky.

It seems that there is an impending storm, as I study the egg drop shaped clouds, with just enough darkness underlining the white. So intrigued am I, as I take this scenery in; however, also recognizing that I am standing solitary, feeling what must seem like loneliness to some, without human voices. The owners of these beautiful boats have not come to sail off into the water today.

I await the sound of birds in the sky, calling out for others to join in finding their first meal from the water. When all of nature is surrounding me, it is a wonderful time to converse with God. He will hear me, even without others around. It is, after all, He who has created these wondrous sights that I now behold. Even in my human aloneness, I feel the love and warmth of Him, while gazing at this gift for all to behold.

A Day with the Dolphins

Around the boat, the dolphins came
Our lives would never be the same
They jumped and spun with such ease
The singing and chanting seemed to please

Soon hundreds more came around
As if mesmerized by the sound
We swam along with our new friends
From human to animal, love transcends

They seemed to understand our souls
Each of us assuming our natural roles
Water, sky, air and sand
A day with the dolphins was so grand

We knew that we could not intrude
Allowing their playful interlude
Soon they allowed us to descend
Into their space until day's end

Memories that will last until we go
A blending of hearts, we now know
Never to forget that special day
When the dolphins came to play

Fire and Ice

Early this morning, the skies entice
Reminding me of fire and ice
Looking out to the dark red hue
But down on the ground, an icy dew

Every day something new to see
Bringing out the awe in me
I see more snow on mountain tops
The beauty and wonder never stops

This is God's promise of a brand new day
He displays it in nature in every way
The quiet of morning, without a sound
A hint of winter approaching on the ground

Seasons come and seasons go
God seems to always put on a show
From an early sunrise to a late sunset
I know I have not seen the best yet

In His way, it is a sign
For me to know, all will be fine
In all things, I give Him my trust
Fire and ice, He has thrust

Seeds of Life

Plant seeds, water and fertilize
Watch your dreams materialize
We start out as a little seed
Added love is what we need

Without this love, we cannot grow
It is hard work, but we must sow
Seeds may not brighten up a room
But suddenly their flowers start to bloom

You must nurture them along the way
Or they will not last another day
When it is cold, you must keep them warm
Bring them inside from the storm

They need more nourishment in the fall
Then they will grow big and tall
Give them attention while they are here
Or in the end you will shed a tear

Seeds of life begin and end
While they are alive, be their friend
One day when you see they wilt
Witness the circle of life without guilt

Love of Nature

From the sea, to the mountain top
My love of nature does not stop
Smelling flowers; watching an eagle fly
So much beauty and I know why

Colored leaves in the fall
Winter's ice on a wall
Birds singing in the spring
For summer's warmth, I do cling

Watching animals as they grow
Plants from seedlings that we sow
In the sky, clouds in my sight
Stars twinkling in the night

After the rain, a bright rainbow
Northern lights put on a show
Sunsets with their colorful hues
With this beauty, I shall not lose

Waves crashing against the rocks
Wind helps sailors to their docks
Night's darkness soon will pass
Morning dew on the grass

The green I see in the trees
It is certain that this does please
I think then, this must be true
Human beings are part of nature too

Snowflake

A snowflake landed on my finger
I wondered how long it would linger
Time stood still; I did not care
I simply held my focused stare

It looked just like a piece of lace
A blanket of white all over the place
Children's laughter was the sound
As they played on snowy ground

I thought about how I felt
As the snow began to melt
An icicle clung to a tree
A feeling of pleasure inside of me

This season will bring out the cold
Soon it will pass; I am told
Part of life passing by
As I looked up to the sky

For the next season, I sit and wait
But for now, I appreciate
This little snowflake in my hand
Just like life, it is so grand

Prisms of Light

Prisms of light on the walls
From the crystal chandelier, to me it calls
At dusk I watch the sun go down
A rainbow of colors removes my frown

Reminding me of the gifts He gave
Like quietly watching an ocean's wave
It only takes a little while
To turn negatives into a smile

Interesting in such a subtle way
To find the silver lining every day
Even when my disappointment grew
Something appeared, showing love so true

Soon I am led to realize
To cut all evil down to size
A sign from God; words from a friend
Showing me blessings that never end

I am learning to watch for the signs
Creases in my face formed from laugh lines
Stars and moon form light so bright
Tomorrow the sun will bring prisms of light

Rainbows and Moonbeams

So many times in my dreams
Behold the rainbows and moonbeams
A part of nature; His Divine gift
My spirits begin to uplift

Colors in rainbows make me sigh
Moonbeams twinkling in the sky
A presence that feels very near
A promise given; so sincere

I look around; what do I see?
The Creator's love surrounding me
Mountains, valleys, lakes and trees
All this beauty is sure to please

Watching wildlife as they play
Seems to make sadness go away
I need not know how or why
I just watch the clouds go by

The crashing of an ocean wave
To see a sunset, is what I crave
A field of flowers with morning dew
His gift of life is so true

Surrendered Thoughts

Surrendered thoughts, my mind set free
Allowing words from inside of me
Pictures that appear in my mind
Not knowing what image I may find

The green foliage on the trees
Fog at sunrise or a summer breeze
An ocean, river, creek or stream
Soon other visions enter my dream

In a rainforest, a pink orchid I see
The crest of a wave or a bud on a tree
Horses galloping below a bluff
Stars, moon, a diamond in the rough

Atop a mountain peak or at the shore
My imagination begins to soar
The clouds turn crimson in the sky
A beautiful sunset makes me sigh

An eagle in flight or a whale at sea
Earth is a fascination to me
Whether on a pier or on island sand
Life for me seems so grand

A deer, a butterfly, clouds and rain
A foamy wave washes away my pain
Hearing a child's infectious laughter
Painting with words is what I am after

Oceans of Life

When I think about the oceans
I see the parallel in my emotions
Rising slowly like the tide
Or against the rocks, waves collide

Thoughts like the water so very deep
Mysterious like secrets that I keep
Looking out when the sea is calm
Feels like reading a comforting psalm

Against my skin, I feel the spray
Quietly then, I sit and pray
Knowing He listens up above
Nurturing me with His great love

Peaceful as when birds take flight
Feeling serene as the moon at night
So many different colors of blue
Always a various change in hue

The lonely call of a humpback whale
Positive goals as I take sail
Continuing to reach for that shore
Until mortal life is no more

Sands of Time

Through the sands of time, off we go
To witness what nature has to show
From the mountains, to the sea
Wildlife, flowers; such ecstasy

Rock formations have been carved
Missing this beauty, I felt starved
God has given us much to see
Praying Mankind has let it be

Cactus, dunes and colors galore
Nature's painting; waiting for more
A waterfall flowing, hard and swift
A bright rainbow; such a gift

Music plays at sunrise
An orange sunset; a sweet surprise
Gazing at stars up in the sky
Wonders of life, and we know why

Seeing an eagle taking flight
Watching whales; what a sight
During our trip, our friendships grow
Taking our time, and going slow

A hush falls upon us late at night
As we observe the bright moonlight
Driving across country, it is so grand
Loving life and our great land

Visions of Pacific Northwest

I listen to the music play
The visions take my breath away
Mountains, rivers and nature's best
All visions of Pacific Northwest

Through a valley, by a stream
Long ago was just a dream
But when you believe as I do
You will see your dreams come true

Never so much beauty have I seen
Blue skies, wildlife and air so clean
From sunrise to sunset I see
The ultimate place on Earth for me

Fog arises with the dew
Peacefulness so serene and true
Crimson clouds in the sky
A winter hawk passes by

A sailboat goes out to sea
Not much better could it be
Sitting atop the mountain high
Close to God, I breathe a sigh

Flight of Fantasy

Far away up into the air
A small plane takes me there
Over the mountains and over the sea
The Greek Isles wait for me

Leaving large cities far behind
Scenic views are on my mind
Slowly flying below the clouds
Far way from bustling crowds

Down below a passing yacht
History and lore, I have been taught
Over ancient ruins; a sight to see
Wonderment of what is to be

A volcano silenced by time
An awesome sunset; so sublime
A lone fisherman with his line cast
Wishing this feeling will forever last

Life stands still as I take in the view
Beautiful dreams can come true
I do not know if this is to be
Flight of fantasy is inside of me

The Blue Hole

I looked up to the sky today
Awaiting God's colors in full array
As if the clouds had a goal
To unmask that large blue hole

Suddenly my biggest wish comes true
As the sunshine starts shining through
The clouds disperse; mountains emerge
My emotions begin to surge

In my heart, I just know
It is God's promise from long ago
I continue to look out for His art
Beautiful impressions in my heart

When I was born, a seed was planted
Nature never taken for granted
The beauty continues to uplift
As God gives us a special gift

I wonder if others take the time
To witness this wonder, so sublime
I thank you God, with my soul
For bringing me to the blue hole

Reflections of Light

Looking across the water to the horizon
I see the sunlight reflecting upon the strait
Its beauty makes me surrender to calmness
The same light reflects in your eyes
That feeling of peacefulness engulfs my soul
It is with this reflection that the parallel between man and nature exist
It is the same as the entire universe has within
We also have this feeling inside, as we are one with that eternal infinity
Light from the sun gives us day time and warmth
A rainbow exists as light is reflected through raindrops
A flickering fire in a campfire or fireplace mesmerizes
Sunlight filters through tall trees
Light creates sunrises and sunsets
The light from a lighthouse guides sailors into shore
The light at the end of a tunnel guides us through the darkness
Light represents ideas, creativity and thoughts
So many positive thoughts come to mind
Thinking of light going on into eternity
I feel that our lives go on that way also
Our mortal bodies may pass, but our spirit is infinity
Reflections of light go on forever

Bounty of Autumn

One of the shortest seasons, yet one of the most beautiful is autumn. After a long hot summer, the season changes, bringing with it cooler temperatures, colored leaves, a bounty of pumpkins and other squash. Children look forward to dressing up in Halloween costumes to collect candy treats. Many of us will sit down and count our blessings at Thanksgiving, sometimes with family or with friends. Kitchens take on the familiar aromas of cinnamon, nutmeg and clove. The scent of turkey roasting in the oven and pumpkin or apple pies baking makes us smile.

It is so exhilarating to take a long drive, sightseeing and taking pictures of trees, where leaves have now turned orange, gold and rust. Sumac grows with its burnt bright red, nestled in amongst green pine trees. Lakes take on a deeper and clearer blue, as birds dip down to catch flies or small fish. Ducks and geese lazily swim, and there is a distant sound of the loon in the background.

Children run and kick large piles of the leaves that have fallen to the ground. The air we breathe in is cool and refreshing. It is the time of year when long walks are taken just to absorb nature's beauty. We have an appreciation for what this season gives us to enjoy, wishing that it would last forever. Soon the trees with be bare, with winter quickly approaching. Squirrels run around collecting as many acorns as they can, knowing that a long winter lies ahead. We wait, wondering if after this enjoyable season, the weather will turn very cold or remain mild. We can only anticipate next year, when again we will behold the bounty of autumn.

Children run and kick large piles of the leaves that have fallen to the ground. The air we breathe in is cool and refreshing. It is the time of year when long walks are taken just to absorb nature's beauty. We have an appreciation for what this season gives us to enjoy, wishing that it would last forever. Soon the trees with be bare, with winter quickly approaching. Squirrels run around collecting as many acorns as they can, knowing that a long winter lies ahead. We wait, wondering if after this enjoyable season, the weather will turn very cold or remain mild. We can only anticipate next year, when again we will behold the bounty of autumn.

Spring a New Beginning

When the last traces of snow begin to disappear, and tiny buds begin to appear on the barren trees, the long anticipated wait for spring is in the making. Birds are busy gathering small twigs and any material they can find to build new nests. Once the new fledglings are born, you can watch them being fed by their mama birds. It will be a while before they try out their wings and take that first flight.

For the first time, heavy winter coats get hung up and light weight jackets can be worn outside. Baby animals begin to be born and the fun of watching ducklings waddle in line behind their mother makes you sigh.

Soon the farmers' market will reopen with a large variety of fresh fruits, flowers, and vegetables, taking the place of what you had to buy at the stores from other places.

Flowers, like tulips show their beautiful colors, enticing you to pick them, then bring inside to enjoy. The lakes and waterways have just cleared of ice and snow, with all of the ice fishing done, and fresh water fishing begins.

This is the season that brings promise of a new beginning. Homes are thoroughly cleaned, and old things are given away or thrown out, making space for new things. The sun begins to shine longer each day, taking the place of the past winter's gray dreariness. Children begin to go outside and play games or ride bikes, scooters, or skates. The air is still crisp at first, but has such a fresh new smell.

Many folks who live on farms start to hang their clothes outside on lines, and the new crops begin to grow. During this season, it is so much more pleasurable to feed the chickens and other farm animals, or take a horseback ride.

Spring allows us to travel with ice free roads, or take a walk in the gentle rain. Everything feels so alive and new. As one of the favorite seasons of the year, spring is seen as life's new beginning.

Sunrise

Sun slowly rising from the east
Shadows fading, clouds dissipating
Mountain tops do now appear
Beauty so profound, in my eyes I see
The reddish hue up in the sky
Birds begin singing their tune
Flowers open their petals slowly
The air is crisp against my skin
Fresh air is what I breathe
Mist clearing at the water's edge
Gentle waves move towards the shore
Seagulls begin their flight
Animals awaken in the morning light
Sun rising higher likened to a yellow ball
Promising another gracious day
My special sunrise music playing
Makes me smile, just knowing
Life has given me one more sunrise

Sunset

Sunlight slowly brings dusk into the sky
The strait waters take on a golden hue
Rocks in the forefront turn from gray to black
The ball of sun turns orange as it sets
The nearby trees now stop swaying
Quietude replaces the daytime noises
The waves make a gentle sound
Slowly, the moon emerges replacing daylight
The gleam on the water mesmerizes my soul
Just standing motionless, watching nature unfold
Watching this day turning to night
Tomorrow sunlight will again bring
The beginnings of what ends in miraculous sunset
Hoping to have many more nights of viewing the splendor
This is God's way of showing that He is near
Letting me know that life's end will be like this
Gentle breezes caressing may face
The mountains become but a shadow
I pray that the sunset of my life is as beautiful

Called to Hurricane Ridge

I wait to go to the mountain top
It beckons to me to never stop
Peace and serenity await me there
When I reach the summit there is not a care

It is here that greenery and snow caps are found
Elk and deer feed on the ground
Looking down at the valley below
Longing for this and needing to go

Clouds and blue sky I can almost touch
My soul needs to be here so very much
Feeling my Creator directly above
When this mountain was made it was done with love

Waiting for me and this I know
This place will cause my happiness to grow
Like a father who is holding his child
My heart is yearning to be in the wild

I take in the surroundings for a long while
Being on that mountain makes me smile
Smelling the clean and crisp fresh air
All I want to do is to stop and stare

My heart feels warm and never cold
As if being taken into His fold
Until I walk over the Heavenly bridge
I am being called to Hurricane Ridge

He Awaits the Muse

Staring far away deep in thought
New ideas were what he sought
Daylight emerged with dawns light
Emotions soon within his sight

As soon as he awoke and left his bed
A symphony entered into his head
Music which has so much feeling
Entered inside and completed the healing

Completely consumed with one song at a time
There is no need to worry about rhyme
First he finds the exact emotion
Each note is played with precise devotion

Using his sense of perfect pitch
With music he makes our hearts so rich
Never promising any exact date
What he gives is worth the wait

He works hard from sunrise to sunset
Music from his heart is what we get
When he is done we cannot refuse
What he creates while he awaits the muse

Inspired by Yanni

Snowfall on Saint James

Sitting in a church one gray day
I just wanted to go out and play
But God must have known my name
From then on I was not the same

Touching my soul, words said to me
My destiny now I could clearly see
Making music I would do
My heart cleansed and now true

Like a whisper from above
God sent down His message of love
Forgot about that fort I wanted to build
On God's path, I was willed

Outside I went, not thinking about fun
Rays on the snow sparkled from the sun
My life changed with no more games
After that snowfall on Saint James

Dance of Passion

Gently being held in your arms
Feeling your embrace and sweet charms
To your music you make me twirl
You make me feel like a young girl

Looking at you makes me blush
I do not let on but keep a hush
Swirling at a very slow pace
A look of passion in your face

Dancing all night to your song
Feeling so right and never wrong
Quietly you look at me with a smile
I know that this will only last a while

Not much longer you will take flight
Holding onto me for what seems all night
Looking at you with no surprise
Love in your heart shows in your eyes

Not a word do you need to say
All that speaks is the music you play
A dance of passion is what you do
Warms my heart through and through

Life's Musical Notes

Think of musical notes on a bar
Now think about your life so far
Some notes are high, some are low
Is this not the way our lives go?

Notes can be flat, or can be sharp
Your words can be kind, or you may yell and harp
Some notes are slow; some go fast
You can smell the roses, or you can speed past

Notes can be quiet, or they can be loud
You can sit alone, or mingle with the crowd
Notes can be serene, or they may pick up speed
You may dance slow, or start wiggling indeed

No matter what notes you play
You have just lived another day
Notes have a beginning and an end
We must pray that more life He will lend

Connections

My mind connecting in all directions
Relating the music after the writing
Feeling totally tuned in
Realizing there must be a cosmic connection
Immersed in the music so totally
Song titles sometimes elude me
Later putting down words subconsciously
Looking back when the music plays
Finding similarities within words and feeling the music
Are they one and the same?
Are the souls joining in complete harmony?
Two arts meet and melt together
Intertwining and interweaving melodies with words
Originating from two separate places
As if both souls and hearts connected
The music moves me then hides in a secret place
Suddenly both music and words make connections

First of August

First of August and there you stand
The look on your face says "life is grand"
Holding onto a branch, reaching for the sky
A happy moment, you cannot deny

Against a background of green leaves
Looking comfortable with rolled up sleeves
Standing there with peace in your eyes
A creative feeling, you cannot disguise

A slight gleam in your eyes, but just a tease
Almost a grin, enough to please
Wondering what is going on inside your head
Speaking of creativity, your words have said

Taking time out from things to do
Words of wisdom coming from you
From the man we know with just one name
Going to the place where we are all the same

Inspired by Yanni

Soothing Music

So soothing does the music play
Wish I could listen the entire day
No words to know what you mean
Only the visions that are seen

Hearing my heartbeat slow way down
Ends the chances of a frown
So quiet and gentle are the notes
Far removed from sowing wild oats

Every note full of emotion
To each element shows devotion
A talent so very unique to you
How I feel, I wish you knew

Such a feeling, I have found
Waiting for that special sound
I anticipate the music's start
A special place in my heart

If you never play another note
Will always love the ones you wrote
If no longer you pursue
The passion remains true to you

You take me to a special place
One that is so full of grace
Cannot imagine how life would be
Without the music inside of me

Inspired by Yanni

Music's Feeling

The sadness of music gives me a feeling
As if it were my heart that it is stealing
My mind soon wanders far away
But in my ears the music must stay

Listening to chords with such intensity
Brings out every bit of my sensitivity
I wait for the momentum to increase
A rush comes over me and does not cease

Then slowly the tempo slows down
My brow will soon lose its frown
My body stays still as I hear it play
But my heart and soul soars without delay

Like a sweet voice talking to me calmly
Every muscle relaxes so serenely
I play it over and over again
I do not want to stop even if I can

You make me laugh; you make me cry
Sometimes you purely make me sigh
Oh what a feeling it is to have the chance
To the music one day, I will stand up and dance

Inspired by Yanni

The Greatest Things

The greatest things seem to be

All those things we receive for free

The love of life is number one

From truth we should never run

The right to create what we choose

With imagination we never lose

Love in our hearts for mankind

Kindness is never hard to find

Showing compassion is the right thing to do

Deep inside of us, these things ring true

Thank you to the one whose quote

Motivated the words that I just wrote

Inspired by Yanni
"The greatest things in life - truth, creativity,
imagination, love, kindness, compassion
are already inside of us, and they're all free."

Intensity

As I look into your eyes
The intensity is no surprise
More music you will now create
I can see you concentrate

Into the black you return
The length of time is no concern
Symphonies dancing inside your head
No time for outside matters to dread

A focused mind in quietude
To this goal you do elude
What you do with total perfection
That stare is your conception

As you go into that place
What comes forth is full of grace
To most, this is not the norm
But we love what you perform

We understand what you do
Your music is so pure and true
To disturb you, we do not dare
Your music you make with great care

Inspired by Yanni

Rekindling of Passion

Like a flame losing its glow
Creative juices that no longer flow
Life seemingly became mundane
Filled your heart up with pain

Through all of the distraction
Came the rekindling of passion
Taking the experience that you know
A different direction, you now go

With sadness, you looked out to the sea
Not knowing how life was to be
Was this now to be the day?
You might throw it all away?

You were on a heavenly mission
When you chose a new position
Now your thoughts begin to center
To a new room, you will enter

It will not be too long
Before you will again become strong
Like the blooming of a crocus
Your mind again will focus

The innocence you once knew
From the light, you withdrew
Return now to the light
Rekindling of passion is within sight

Inspired by Yanni

Into the Black

I close my eyes into the black
Where imagination has no lack
I relax my mind, and then I wait
Writing words before too late

Music conjures images in my mind
Suddenly right words I do find
Getting thoughts to paper real fast
Before the feeling would have passed

At times the feeling is so strong
Thoughts sometimes short, sometimes long
Not so sure if it makes sense
The feeling at that moment so intense

Sometimes I write late at night
Or the muse might enter at morning's light
Never knowing what may emerge
It comes forth like a lightning surge

With these feelings I do not judge
At that time, not needing a nudge
May not know how it will turn out
In the black there is no self doubt

Seasons

Winter, spring, summer, fall
Something to love about all
Count the seasons, there are four
When one ends, we still have more

Winter filled with cold and snow
Chilly winds outside do blow
Bundled up to meet the day
Children going out to play

Spring arrives, flowers grow
New life begins, this we know
Birds sing, buds on the trees
Warm sunshine soon will please

Summer filled with the sun's heat
Keeping cool is such a treat
To the mountains and to the shore
Having fun is what's in store

Fall comes filled with colored leaves
Hues of gold, orange, rust on trees
Squirrels scurry for their food
Crisp air puts us in good moods

Something special in each season
Loving each for a different reason
Looking forward to life's changes
Our Creator forever rearranges

Based on "Seasons" by Yanni

Voyage

Life began like a voyage upon the sea
Uncharted courses, the vessel takes me
From innocence of my path unknown
Through the years, my life has grown

From bright sunshine and skies so blue
To dark clouds and storms I knew
Although I have gone through torrential rain
I have survived through pleasure and pain

Traveling the sea of calm and peace
My faith of love would never cease
I would look up to the sky
Watching a beautiful eagle fly

A journey of promise sent from above
Feeling the constant unconditional love
Life has hurdles along the way
No more than I can handle, I heard Him say

When things seem too hard to bear
The music can take me anywhere
Spreading the message that we are one
The love chain will not come undone

Listen closely; can you hear it?
It is the sound of your inner spirit
Continuing faith in what may be
Until this voyage ends for me

Inspired by "Voyage" by Yanni

Mission of Love

They serve their country to protect our land
Sent to the jungles and into the sand
They pray for protection from above
As our military is on a mission of love

We may not pick them out in a crowd
But knowing what they do, should make us proud
Soldiers who put their lives on the line
Families and friends praying for a positive sign

Sometimes it is hard for them to cope
They need us to fill their minds with hope
We reach into our heart, and try to give
Prayers and love, as long as they live

We need to show them, that what they do
For their efforts, our support is true
Praying music and words take away their pain
The freedom we have, is what we gain

For all of the men and women out there
Please know how much we truly care
Let these words reach you with love
Praying for your safety, from the Creator above

Commitment of Unconditional Love

They have taken an oath, a commitment to serve
They know not what may be around each curve
Forward they go, taking all in their stride
Serving our country with love and great pride

Though the danger they face, may be grand
They show no fear in protecting our land
Loved ones send them off with a wave
Praying for each life that they save

No longer are their heads in a cloud
They have a purpose, of which we are proud
Each day, as our flag is unfurled
We pray for peace all around the world

Around the globe, men and women roam
Making it safe for us at home
A comfort to know that they are there
Whether by sea, land, or air

When they are away, they serve and protect
When they return, they deserve respect
For all of those, who serve us at home,
In our hearts, you too are dear

Many men and women have retired
Through the years, you have been admired
We thank all of you and the Creator above
For your commitment of unconditional love

Love Letters From Afar

Late at night, he got up from his cot, and quietly went over to a table, with a tablet and pen in his hand. In the dark of night, all seemed to have quieted down, after a day of fighting, far away from home. His comrades were all asleep, as it appeared that the enemy slept as well; so he took this time to sit down, with the soft glow of a lamp, and wrote a letter to his dear wife.

It was important to write to her as often as he felt safe to do so. Sending and receiving letters seemed to be the one thing that kept his spirits and hopes of survival alive. With each new day, when he arose from slumber, he felt grateful to his Creator, that he was allowed another day. He prayed that it would be one less day of fighting; that soon he would be called to go home to his lovely wife. That night, while he wrote the letter, he was listening to beautiful and inspiring music from his CD player. The music seemed to soothe away his troubled heart, and relaxed his mind. This helped him to write encouraging and positive words which would ease her mind as well.

As he wrote, he reflected on how warm the fire felt during winter time at home. He and his wife snuggled close to one another, feeling the warmth of the fire; while being mesmerized by the flicker of the flames. Their love for each other, so deep; but they both understood that each of these days together might be the last for a while, as soon he would be called away to serve his country. They savored each and every precious moment in time.

Early one morning, she awoke thinking about the day she had to say goodbye to her wonderful husband. Before he boarded the large transport plane, they held each other for what seemed like an eternity. A promise was made to write to each other every day; or at least she would, before going to work. They kissed each other goodbye; then she watched him walk away towards the plane. They both agreed that they would pray daily for his safe return; as well as for peace amongst all of mankind.

That evening, she sat in front of the fireplace, listening to music that filled the room. The soft glow of the flames took her back to a special time, when they sat together. They talked about wanting a family, but decided to wait until he returned from the war. They both wanted to be together to share each moment up to, during and after the birth. She prayed that he would return home, so that this dream would become a reality. She had to remain in a positive frame of mind; not doubting that her husband would be protected from harm. Each morning, her letters to him were always uplifting and happy. She refused to show any sadness in her heart, so that he would smile and keep looking forward to their future together.

When she came home from work every day, she would anxiously await the mailman's delivery, hopeful for a letter from abroad. Every now and then, a letter would be delivered later in the day, as her carrier knew how much she looked forward to her husband's letters. He loved to surprise her by making a second appearance at her door, with a letter he found in the late mail. This always put a special smile on her face. The letters were what kept her happy, as well as kept her hopes alive, just like her husband's.

One day, he was summoned by his superior officer, and given a notice of his release from his tour of duty overseas. The war was now declared over, and he along with others would be going home. He happily gathered up his belongings; amongst those were loving letters from his wife. Upon his arrival, his wife rushed to him, embracing him with great joy. They went home, and she brought out a decorative box, which held all of his letters. He added the letters that he had saved from her. This treasured memory box now contained both of their love letters from afar.

Still the Same

With a body broken, home he came
But heart and soul are still the same
Off to war, he walked erect
He still deserves your respect

You should not stop and stare
Instead show him you still care
Nothing has changed in his heart
Because he cannot dodge and dart

When he left, you had such pride
Please do not let your feelings hide
Inside that body, remains his soul
Life changes with a different goal

Somewhere out there is a dove
Who protected him with her love
Go beyond what your eyes see
He is the best that he can be

You knew the dangers that he faced
With conviction, from harm he raced
Life does not hold guarantees
It may not happen as we please

Look down deeper inside his eyes
For they do not hold a disguise
His heart and soul play no game
Inside he is still the same

Praying For Peace

This morning I looked at my reflection
Praying to Him for your protection
Wishing for the fighting to cease
All I want to know is peace

What you do, I so admire
A homecoming is my desire
So far away, it seems so sad
Would loving each other be so bad?

I think so much about your plight
I think of you late at night
I pray that it will not be too late
Before you get your return date

For now, please look to Him above
Sending you a blanket of love
Know that my respect is true
Pray before your day is through

It is with you that I believe
With Him, your faith will relieve
Praying for all to get along
Praying that you will stay strong

Children of Love

From our wonderful God above
We all are his children of love
There was no second guessing
When He gave us this blessing

One generation leads to two
Bringing forth more love as He would do
Even when our children cry and fuss
They always mean so much to us

While we watch them grow up and play
We know that eventually they will move away
Then the circle of love begins
More children to love and everyone win

There is no way that we can hide
The love and joy we have inside
For those of us who have given birth
There is no price for what they are worth

Enjoy your children while you can
They each grow up to be a lady or a man
There are no words that can really say
How children of love can make your day

A Kiss at Sunrise

When darkness leaves the night time skies
From you, a kiss at sunrise
In everything you seem to do
I receive your love so true

I have felt from the start
In your eyes, love from the heart
Walking through time, hand in hand
Feeling inside that life is grand

From the mountains to the shore
We could not love any more
Through rain or sun, day or night
We have found a love so right

As you lay right next to me
The utmost love is what I see
Then our lips soon do meet
Our souls entwined, we won't retreat

Arms surround with loving care
Through all time, we will share
Another day, looking in your eyes
Returning a kiss at sunrise

Expressions of Love

The word 'Love' encompasses a multitude of definitions. Most people immediately think of the romantic exchanges between two people in love with each other, including passionate interludes.

However, love can be so much more than that, including feelings for humankind in general. Friendships form bonds that can boggle the mind, and excludes logic, especially when these bonds exist without having had direct contact.

I have pondered on how these special relationships can evoke such a deep form of love and caring. These are the feelings of having brothers and sisters far removed from blood lines. When people care enough to respect, love and comfort people, without wanting anything in return, this profound love must be recognized as being just as special as those formed in marriages or family ties. They bear just as much importance, with thoughts of unselfish and unconditional giving.

The world becomes a better place in which to live, love and share those invisible feelings we each have inside ourselves. To give love in this manner is to receive the greatest gift. It is so simple, yet sometimes so difficult to understand. It is something that resides deep inside each one of our souls, and should be given and exchanged from inside our hearts freely.

When Two Souls Join As One

From the heavens and out from the stars
Two who are meant for one another soon meet
Their hearts seem to be the same
When two souls join as one

It may take years or decades to happen
But when the time is right
They stare into each other's eyes for the very first time
Somehow it feels like they have known each other for an eternity

True love cannot be rushed or forced
Like nature's cycles, or like the waves in an ocean
Each one must be timed and nurtured
Life grooms us for our significant other

At times it seems as if it may not happen
Suddenly, the emergence of that special someone
Lets you know that it was worth the long wait
A special gift has been given of great worth

Like learning to walk, before we can run
Each step must be taken with care and patience
Hearts may be broken; losses may occur
Each hurdle; another lesson learned

Love being the ultimate shared gift
The best emotion to be shared by two
Out from the dark clouds, it seems
Sunshine will fill our hearts with warm rays

When we least expect it to happen
There will be a beautiful stranger

The appearance of our perfect soul mate
It is at that time when two souls join as one

Outpouring of Love

God knows when we are in need
He works through us to do His deed
We are His vessel not to be confused
Spreading His love is how we are used

When we feel down or very hurt
He puts His angels on high alert
He lets us know that He is there
He returns joy to us with great care

Our dues have long ago been paid
Friends will soon come to our aid
Then it only takes a while
Back on our faces returns the smile

It is alright sometimes to feel sad
With little effort we soon will feel glad
Just allow His angels to talk
Go outside and take a walk

Each time it happens you will be stronger
The pain in your heart remains no longer
I have to thank the Creator above
For sending this healing outpouring of love

A Path with Heart

A path with heart is what I have chosen
Even when the road is frozen
In a world filled with wrath
I will continue on God's path

Loving people as I go
With His love, this I know
Wanting nothing more than to give
He has shown me how to live

My heart seems to be at peace
Since the day I allowed release
Walking happily mile by mile
Passing folks with a smile

Watching the trees gently sway
Being grateful for another day
Looking at the clouds up above
Feeling that invisible sign of love

Another day given is worth living
Always more chances for giving
Asking Him where else to start
He shows me a path with heart

Empowered by Love

When you feel weak instead of strong
Stop and think of a beautiful song
Visualize a white turtle dove
Start feeling empowered by love

Life may seem a little wild
Remember back like an innocent child
Do not look at life feeling forlorn
Be perfect as before you were born

Look at a baby's sweet smile
Your worries will cease in a while
Surround yourself with positive friends
The spirit in you never ends

See yourself with what you desire
Soon you will find that you are higher
Thank your Creator in advance
Success happens when given the chance

Enjoy each day for what you reap
One goal at a time is all you keep
Do not fear, but stand up tall
Empowered by love, you have all

Motivated by Love

Sharing, praying and fulfilling needs
Motivated by love causes these deeds
All of these things come in a natural way
For these things, no one should repay

To see someone heal, be happy or smile
Makes what is done very worthwhile
When what is inside a heart is true
All things given come naturally to you

Everything deep down was sent from above
No longer is it difficult to share our great love
Untapped emotions now being released
Holding back feelings have forever ceased

Watching miracles happen keeps us motivated
Positive results keeps hearts satiated
In life giving can never be too late
A receptive audience is what we await

Message in a Bottle

As I take a walk along the sea
Profound feelings deep inside of me
How do I get a message out to you?
Hoping it will somehow get through

Knowing you are across this land
As I make footprints in the sand
Feelings hidden so long ago
To be revealed so that you know

As I watch the seagulls cross the sky
Remembering your departure, I have to cry
Special moments spent with you
Hoping that you miss me too

I could not tell you how I feel
But these feelings are so real
Secrets hidden deep inside my heart
I just don't know where to start

With a pen and paper, I start to write
Been thinking of you day and night
Writing thoughts to help me heal
Peace that the night seems to steal

An old bottle washes up on shore
This is the answer I was searching for
This vessel will hold my message inside
As the ocean takes it with the tide

Although I know not where you are
My message in the bottle will travel far
Perhaps God will be its guide
Praying you find it on the other side

Green Machine

Remember when to get things clean
You were told to buy the "Green Machine"?
We bought it before it was too late
We wondered why we did not wait

Yes, it vacuumed with such power
But its weight turned us sour
Our bodies went through so much pain
Pushing that monster was insane

When we could not take any more
We returned it to the store
No longer the beast, we would fight
"Give us a vacuum that is light"

A tiny one then, we did buy
When it did not work, we wondered why
Into the closet it did go
So what if a little dust does show?

One day the bags got too old
Now the bag less ones were sold
Different colors, we did try
No matter what, vacuums make me cry

Chicken Soup

Through the years, when I got a cold
My mom would serve the soup of gold
That would throw germs for a loop
Because there is magic in chicken soup

This one thing makes it clear
Memories of "Mom" are still dear
She rarely needed to take a look
At any recipe, for her to cook

So much about her that I miss
Aromas in her kitchen was pure bliss
Learned how to cook when we were poor
I just want to beg for more

So much from her that I learned
For her cooking, I have still yearned
I stand by the stove, and often smile
Her spirit stands with me for awhile

As my life goes on, I want to strive
To keep those memories in me alive
Next time I start to feel a sneeze
Some chicken soup will surely please

Mile Wide Smile

It is so nice, once in a while
On someone's face, a mile wide smile
A sparkle appears in their eyes
Happiness you cannot disguise

Like the sun shining bright
Pulling others into their light
A glow appears on their face
Joy spreads all over the place

Smiles at times, lead to laughter
Making it last 'til ever after
Start smiling when you wake up
Put pure love into your cup

When you smile, others feel good
Keep that emotion, just as you should
A true smile never tells lies
A happy nature is no surprise

A smile is a very good way to start
Soon happy feelings warm your heart
You attract so many with your style
Practice daily that mile wide smile

Sticky Notes

A note here, an address there
In the drawer, a sticky note where?
Something specific, I need to know
I ask myself, "Where did it go?"

So convenient, in many sizes
What is written brings surprises
Such a bad habit, it makes me smile
As I sort through a large pile

Of course the one I am looking for
Has gotten misplaced in that drawer
I mean to put them in a book
But in the drawer, I still look

Yellow, pink and sometimes blue
Jotting on them is what I do
Someday I will find a better way
For now my sticky notes save the day

Little Things

Sunshine, smiles, rainbows, butterflies
Clouds, animals, babies and skies
Laughs, sighs, music, a bird's wings
Happiness found in those little things

A warm puppy, a purring kitten
Watching snowflakes land on your mitten
Giving love and hearing a thank you
Hearing someone say I love you

A hug, a kiss or tender touch
Warms your heart so very much
Smelling flowers, enjoying the sun
It is so simple for you to have fun

Hearing a baby say its first word
The most beautiful sound you ever heard
Making new friends every day
Looking forward to the first of May

Listening carefully to your Source
A new destiny will chart life's course
Count your blessings and your heart sings
Always appreciate those little things

Magic Carpet Ride

In my mind I dip and glide
Traveling on a magic carpet ride
Above the city's thunderous roar
My heart at peace forevermore

Any place I wish to go
Happiness on my face does show
To any land far away
I take this ride so I can play

My face now has a glow
New friends I now do know
By myself or amongst the crowds
Soaring high above the clouds

Imagination with nothing to hide
Anyone can join in this ride
Even if only for a little while
Always keeping that special smile

Given chances to clearly see
Locked up deep inside of me
Like a never ending rope
This journey is filled with hope

Ride with me and take my hand
Sitting side by side in the sand
Understanding what we should
In all of us there is good

Imagination

To have imagination means owning a wonderful possession. The possibilities are never ending. Think about everything one can do in the world of creativity.

You can climb the highest mountain without fear of falling. Imagine yourself sitting atop the highest peak of the most beautiful mountain in the world, without suffering from the bitter cold. You can sit there for hours while taking in the snow, wildlife, flora, and fauna. You can take in the wispy clouds and the blue sky as never seen before. You can see the world below with complete clarity.

You can swim in the pristine ocean waters without fear of drowning or being hurt by predators. Imagine the feel of the ocean spray on your face as you sit in the sand, watching the otters, seals, dolphins, and whales swim and play in the deep blue water. Swim below the ocean depths, and experience the beauty of coral and underwater plants. See yourself watching the most beautiful sunset over the quieting waves, while awaiting the moon's silver shimmer on the water at night.

Traveling anywhere in or out of the world is possible by any mode of transportation. You can take a cruise to Greece, or anywhere by sea. Take a flight to the furthest corners of the earth. Drive across the entire country. You can even become an astronaut and see the earth from space, knowing that a safe return is guaranteed.

With your imagination running freely, you can explore and travel anywhere, anytime, in the past, present or future. You are not bound by any limitations of where your mind travels in your imaginary world. It is here where pain, sadness and adversity cease to exist. You can chart your own destiny. By using your imagination, you can have endless fantasies. Enjoy the ride and explore your creative mind.

Recipe for a Smile

When people I encounter ask me, "How are you?" I respond with "Excellent!" with a great deal of enthusiasm. I have been very amazed at how many people have had a look of utter surprise or shock on their faces. One girl stopped what she was doing, looked at me and exclaimed, "What did you say?" Another cashier said to her coworker, "Did she just say excellent?" It is almost as though most people expect answers, for example, I'm fine, okay, so-so, not too bad, but the word excellent rings like a foreign word to them. The end result is usually what I'm hoping for however...a smile! I figure that if I can leave someone smiling, I have done my job for the day.

We currently live in a world filled with turmoil, such as wars, violence, fear, loss of employment, homes being foreclosed upon, and a myriad of negative attitudes and actions, not to mention natural disasters on our planet. One might think that with all of this occurring, how can I or anyone else maintain a positive attitude, and see the light at the end of the tunnel. For the most part, I have usually always been a fairly positive person, but in the last decade, events caused me to reassess my life and attitudes; thereby adopting the most positive way of looking at life as I possibly could. I intend on sharing what I practice with anyone and everyone who wants to read or listen to what I have to say. I have been on a long journey, spanning over six decades, with a lot of hills and valleys, just like everyone else. I hope by sharing much of how I attained my positive attitude, that others will find inner peace as well.

Life for everyone has its ups and downs, good and bad, happiness and sadness. I do not know of anyone who has had a perfect, idyllic life, void of problems now and then.

I have had my share of both ends of that spectrum, and during those down times, could have easily succumbed to giving up, being negative, or not looking forward to creating the life I preferred. Fortunately I acquired a wealth of knowledge, as well as alternative ways of looking at the hurdles of life.

I remember more of the negative events in my life of course, as those always stand out, and at times have a greater effect on our memory. I recall everything from my parents fighting with each other, and taking their frustrations out on my brother and me. In school, at times because I was short and small, the other children picked on me, or got into fights with me. This ultimately forced me to become stronger, and I learned to fight back to protect myself. As a young adult, and after ending my first marriage, I went through a great deal of trauma from several men being sexually violent. The list of my emotional roller coaster ride continued to be a part of my life's journey.

The negatives in my life began to add up and take its toll on my self-esteem. I felt that I was never good enough, unsuccessful at following anything through, would not see my dreams come true, or amount to anything considered worthy. I believe that many people go through these negative emotions, only questioning "why me"?

Through doing a lot of soul searching, reading, listening to people with positive philosophies, I was able to leave my dungeon of doubts about myself, raise myself up to believing that I could be the person that I was born to be, follow my dreams no matter how small, and pass my positive attitude and smile to others. If I can do this, I truly believe anyone can do this as well.

In Your Direction

You have reached down and touched my soul. I have found peace, love and serenity. You are guiding and walking by my side. I will listen with my heart to your words, as they enter into my mind, showing me the way to my destination. I know that only you can provide me with my needs, my nourishment, my mission in life, my physical and spiritual healing. I claim what is rightfully mine, not in ego or selfishness, but solely to fulfill your purposes for me.

I will be all that I will be, knowing that I can and will go above and beyond those things that I never humanly knew were possible. You hold the map of where I am to go, where I am to be, what I am to do for others. I go diligently, obediently and lovingly, with a smile caressing my face, warmth inside my heart, and hope for all of Mankind.

In your direction, I will find all of what I thought was lost. I will know that all wrong will become right because of your deep, never ending love. I will commit to do everything in your will for me. I will be the light that you send down from the sun. I will shine like the stars you have provided in the night's sky. I will be the rainbow that emerges after the rain. I will be the blue sky after the storm.

I now live my life in your beautiful reflection, as it was meant to be from the beginning of time. I will promise to have patience that all things happen in your time, and never in my own. May I wake up daily and walk in faith, no matter where I go, or what I may do. You are my Creator; you are my wisdom, and my loving guide. You are the owner of my spirit, my heart, my destiny, my soul.

When You Believe

When you believe, dreams can come true
Miracles are possible; do not be blue
See yourself at the end of the rainbow
In your heart, make beauty all you know

Life's negativity will try to get you down
But we must try to reverse our frown
Look outside and see life grow
Know that you will reap what you sow

Your life has always belonged to God
Remove the rocks on which you trod
Pull all the love inside of you
Give it out no matter what you do

You attract in life what you say
Keep looking forward to each new day
Before you know it, you will see
The place where you would like to be

Against all odds, you can break through
Because He also believes in you
As you face the dark tunnel with dread
See the light emerging for you ahead

When you believe, you will start to smile
Because smiling takes just a little while
Happiness fights all those foes
Your hopes and dreams bring sweet repose

Road Leading to Love

While traffic tries to push and shove
Take the road leading to love
So much beauty to behold
See your path paved with gold

Beside the pavement you will find
Nature's glory entering your mind
A lot of things to see and do
Protective arms will see you through

Passing through mountains and prairies
Your passengers are angels and fairies
Beautiful music playing in your ears
Miles go by without any fears

Across the country you will go
Bringing you happiness; this I know
Soon you will be amongst friends
Your road leading to love never ends

Led By Spirit

I have begun to hear it
I am being led by Spirit
Words being fed into my mind
To me, my Creator is so kind

Doing what I would not dare
Now I write without a care
Music, pictures, words help me
Visions in my mind, I clearly see

Talent that only comes from above
He is filling me with His love
Allowing me to share with you
What I now love to do

Following instructions from Him
I do not write merely on a whim
My life feels like a sweet song
Wishing I could write all day long

I write, led by Spirit and His grace
He takes me to a Divine place
No longer a life of wrath
I now follow in His path

Sunshine in Your Heart

I hardly know where I should start
Writing about sunshine in your heart
Instead of seeing skies of gray
Inside, find sunshine every day

Do not see darkness like a shroud
Find the beauty in each cloud
After the rains come, look up high
See the rainbow in the sky

The sky changes with a different hue
Look at leaves with drops of dew
About God's love, you will declare
Smell the freshness in the air

There will always be another day
For you to go outside and play
Each cloud outside has a style
Enough to make you sit and smile

Although the sunshine, you may adore
Sunny days will emerge once more
Grass and plants have much to gain
When God sends His gentle rain

Life has cycles, like rain and snow
Spring brings sunshine; then things grow
New life then begins to start
Always keep sunshine in your heart

Back to Center Core

When you think that life can give you no more
It is time for you to go back to center core
God gives you the choices for you to choose
It is up to you whether you win or you lose

When troubles find you, and you shut Him out
Allowing you to fill your heart with hurt and doubt
Instead of letting yourself become weak
It should be His love that you now seek

It is not necessary to see the proof
Listen carefully to Him for the truth
Do not let Evil take hold of you
Take control of your thoughts in all you do

No matter how difficult your plight may be
He knows your needs and will let you see
Take all of the hurt, pain and wrath
Let Him guide you to the right path

In the dark tunnel, look towards the light
Soon your life's mission will feel right
Shove the Evil outside your door
Reach deep down back to center core

Colors

Like a rainbow after the rain
All of us have an aura just the same
Each of us has a different hue
One color is distinctly you

We color with crayons as a child
Some are subtle and some are wild
When we get older we color with paint
Some like bold and some like faint

For those of us lucky enough to see
Different colors we can be
Even so we are the same inside
That is one thing we cannot hide

Music can evoke different colors too
In our imagination this is true
Dark colors seen late at night
Turn to gold and red in the sunlight

We are each as individual as can be
Put together we are beautiful you see
An artist blends colors on a board
A picture full of color is the reward

Look Towards the Light

Look towards the light and you will see
Hope, peace and serenity
Sunny rays make you feel good
A smile appears as it should

All good things come in time
Rushing can feel like such a crime
Take a breath of clean fresh air
Remove worry and take good care

When you come to that place of doubt
Walk away and throw that out
Slowly go back to your special place
Creativity will be full of grace

If darkness brings sadness and great pain
Cloudy days with storms and rain
Wait for the sunrise in the sky
You will realize the reasons why

Do not always go looking back
All you will see is what you lack
Look ahead and wear a smile
Happiness will return in a little while

Giving Divine Direction

My Creator in His perfection
Is giving me Divine direction
Though what path I do not know
I trust that this He will show

Through the music He speaks to me
Changing me into what He wants me to be
I just have to listen and make myself hush
He slows me down from life's rush

When I come to that fork in the road
He will decide for me, removing my load
Like a piece of clay being molded
His plan for me is being unfolded

Coming out of my human wrath
I now follow my new path
He will employ me for His needs
Allowing me to share good deeds

Listening carefully to what I hear
I know I will find peace very near
For now I will hold on tight
As He takes me on a Divine flight

New Beginning

Life is giving me a new beginning
Like a race that I am winning
A new adventure has begun
I look forward to having fun

So much ahead now will unfold
Like a new road paved in gold
No longer at an age to dread
Like a child, I look ahead

So much beauty, I now see
Fear and doubt, not a part of me
Every day I thank Him so
For giving me a place to go

I wake up with a brand new start
With nothing but happiness in my heart
In humbleness, I ask Him what to do
Every day is so brand new

I do not dwell on what I lack
I no longer wish to look back
To forge ahead, in faith I know
My confidence now continues to grow

A change in life is very near
Nothing inside left to fear
To serve, I give all my best
A new beginning; a brand new quest

Colors of Pompoms

What color would you choose your pompoms to be?
Red, yellow, green or blue like the sea
Purple, white orange or pink
A reflection of you is what I think

The colors of pompoms for Him I know
Would be all of the colors in a rainbow
That is how I see His gift
Rainbow colored pompoms that uplift

Let us stand together and give Him a cheer
For us, He will always be near
Cheerleading angels all over the place
Continually showing us His sweet grace

Heavenly cheerleaders from above
Showering each of us with their love
It does not matter what color you choose
With these pompoms, you cannot lose

Jump, cheer and sing a song
Help each other get along
One day we meet at Heaven's gate
Cheer for each other before it is too late

If I Were a Rainbow

If I were a rainbow up in the sky
I would reach across and make you smile
Bright colors would release your sigh
Pain replaced by happiness in just a while

If I were a rainbow I would reach for you
My spectrum surrounding you with sweet caress
Soon you would see blue skies too
Taking you away from all duress

If I were a rainbow with a pot of gold
You would feel His love so true
Bright colors appearing so bold
Following you with all you do

If I were a rainbow, would you follow me?
Feel the love and pass it around
Look beyond now; soon you will see
From end to end, removing that frown

If I were a rainbow in all my glory
After the storm a promise is made
From my light, will emerge a story
Keep watching until you see me fade

Pretty Paper

On pretty paper; words from the heart
A design is chosen; then thoughts start
Parchments, textures, different hues
Blue skies, water, rainbows fuse

Themed paper carefully chosen
Along with feelings, shows emotion
Soon words flow at full sail
Before it's sent through the mail

Hoping to make the reader soar
One could not ask for more
Words replace a gentle touch
Feeling the love, of which there's much

Picking ink colors and type of font
A perfect blending is what we want
One can only hope and pray
Understanding from far away

When one cannot be right here
Sometimes we just shed a tear
When sadness emerges late at night
Writing on pretty paper feels so right

The Source

Like the truth revealed
The Source is never concealed
Open your heart
It is where you start

Dreams will come true
It is inside of you
You know where it came from
Like a beat of a drum

Love will abide
If you let Him inside
What was once tucked away
Will emerge strong today

Give thanks to the One above
He shares His great love
Inspiration comes through
Revealed by the Source just for you

Beacon of Light

A lighthouse shines a beacon of light
Guiding sailors to shore safely at night
Like an angel's protection used to guide
The light not allowing land to hide

Our Creator protects us much the same way
Shining sun's light during the day
Later at night we see the moonlight
Keeping us from darkness or having fright

Lighthouses standing strong through the ages
Often found written about on writers' pages
Visitors climb to the top of her stairs
Looking out to sea, removing all cares

Lighthouses seem to draw out the curious
Tales often make them seem so mysterious
Like God's promises, one can guarantee
Lighthouses watched from out in the sea

Learning Curve

Life is much like a learning curve
To avoid hazards we must swerve
Just when we think we are on a roll
Events happen that are out of our control

Even when things seem to go wrong
This is when our faith must make us strong
We cannot allow the evil one's wrath
To take us away from our chosen path

Hurt and pain may make us grieve
But soon a peaceful feeling will come to relieve
Our future may be uncertain as to which way to go
With open minds our destiny we shall know

Like sailing along in an uncharted sea
We let ourselves calm down so we can just be
We hold on to those dear to our heart
Never fearing when the unknown will start

We look at each day as something brand new
Like an adventure you will be shown what to do
Embark on your journey with little concern
Ask with your heart what you will now learn

Perpetual Motion

When standing still life continues to go on in perpetual motion
When we feel as if we are alone people still walk around us
When we feel the door close behind us someone will open it later
When one heart stops beating another will just begin
When one flower wilts another bud will start to open
When a tree is cut down another will be planted
When someone moves away somebody will move in
When we lose one love another will replace it
When we think our hearts are full we will find more space
When we feel we can no longer love we will find a way to give more
When we feel like not going on someone will help us go further
When we think we have lost hope something will change our minds
When we feel creativity has eluded us the muse will enter inside
When we try to open our minds the truth will enter
When we think of ourselves as unworthy someone will point out our best
When we take our last breath we will have given life the best we had

Acceptance

Walking through life never having faith in oneself can lead to unfulfilled dreams, missed opportunities and all hope of achieving our goals. It is only when suddenly there is a ray of hope that enters our minds, allowing us to soar above all our own expectations, that we truly see who we really are.

We enter a realm of acceptance which allows us to soar, ignoring imperfection. No longer are we afraid to do what was only in our imagination. Instead we believe in ourselves enough to break the boundaries and barriers.

Our hearts, minds and souls are set free, with a sense of well being, hope, and happiness. We now are allowed to experience adventure, imagination and creativity. No longer do we say "I cannot do this, because I am not good enough". We turn our attitude into knowing that we can now do anything we make up our minds to accomplish. We now walk through our lives with pride, confidence and self-acceptance.

Destiny of the Heart

Goals, dreams and aspirations held inside your heart are just waiting to be freed.

When you believe that what you want to achieve can be obtained, and that miracles do truly happen, anything is possible.

You must allow your thoughts to be turned into reality, simply by visualizing, knowing and feeling that all of us are capable of turning what is locked inside our minds and hearts is truly possible.

To start out just the same as a baby learns to take its first step; you must begin slowly until each action becomes an automatic reaction.

You must follow your heart's path, as hearts do not lie.

Search for the truth which is locked inside, allowing your soul to fly freely and discover its potential.

Once the truth is revealed, allow yourself to totally believe, never wavering, as you see your dreams become real and concrete.

Soon you will realize that when what you imagine and believe is true, nothing is beyond your realm of achievement.

Confidence levels rise, and you will no longer find it difficult to reach for the stars.

See yourself with what you want, or where you wish
to be each and every day until it materializes.

Realize that if something is meant to be, you can
make it become true.

Nothing is more fulfilling than obtaining happiness
by following the destiny of the heart.

Heightened Senses

Sometimes my heart sheds a tear
No longer whispers do I hear
Long ago I really could
Quiet words, I understood

I watch expressions and I read
I get the knowledge that I need
I may not hear all the birds
I now hear music without words

My other senses, I can use
Giving up, I just refuse
I look at things a different way
Although I hear not what they say

My eyes still see the bright sunlight
My hands can still hold you tight
I still have my sense of smell
What you are cooking, I can tell

I used to dwell about the cost
About the sense that I had lost
But now I finally realize
I have touch, smell, taste and eyes

These heightened senses inside of me
The beauty of nature, I can see
So much enjoyment, I have found
I still love life without sound

Never Stop Dreaming

Never stop dreaming from your heart
Thinking positively is a very good start
It may be hard to do what you should
Keep all of your thoughts pure and good

Keep a smile and give a shout
Tell the world, you have no doubt
A new adventure; a brand new chance
This should make you sing and dance

Practice daily, and in a while
No one will remove your smile
Love one another with all your might
One by one, we can make things right

Put that smile upon your face
Spreading happiness all over the place
Make sure to share your kindest word
The best thing folks have ever heard

Love is free, and the greatest gift
With this richness, you uplift
When someone feels like they are down
Pass some kindness, not a frown

Once you show how much you care
Your own wishes, you can share
Never stop dreaming, as He hears you
Soon your dreams will come true

Blessings of Thanksgiving

There are many blessings of Thanksgiving
Treasure each day that you are living
Awake and think about a way
How to brighten someone's day

At the stores, some push and shove
Take some time to share some love
Some out there do not have food
Help them have a better mood

As we sit and have our meal
Think of how the homeless feel
Many are very far away
No family to celebrate Thanksgiving Day

Stop and think before you groan
What it feels like to be all alone
Stand up, and sing and shout
So much to be happy about

Life is short; it is true
Keep gratefulness inside of you
The next time you sit and pray
Thank Him for blessing you today

Words You Utter

Take caution in what you say
It might determine the price you pay
Negative thoughts will put you down
Positive thoughts will remove the frown

Look at yourself in a positive light
Practice this with all of your might
See yourself with good health
Believing can also control your wealth

See beauty everywhere along your path
Do not be hateful or practice wrath
You are perfect in every way
The Source created you with love that day

Words you utter can connect with spirit
Know that someone nearby will hear it
Sadness, hurt and pain will not return
If only pure words you now learn

Forgive your enemies for their mistakes
Use the love that your heart makes
You will attract what you feel
Words you say will become real

Use nature's creations as your guide
Soon you will take things in stride
Remove ego and use self control
Smiles and happiness are now your goal

Depth Perception

Truth lies deeper than the skin
You must look beyond and from within
Beauty can be on the outside
But the interior must be your guide

A rock can seem completely strong
But standing below might find you wrong
Look into the eyes deep to the soul
For evil may lurk and destroy your goal

Keep your senses on high alert
False smiles and promises may just be a flirt
Your ears must be tuned to get good reception
With clarity soon you will have depth perception

Every day learn something new
You will recognize whose heart is true
Absorb and obtain all of the facts
The day will come to have fun and relax

Facing the Unknown

Often fearful seeds are sown
When we are facing the great unknown
Soon doubt and worry begin to show
Nervousness soon begins to grow

We must have faith in things unsaid
Otherwise hope turns to dread
If we are truly God's reflection
He will lead us in the right direction

Worrying gives us nothing to gain
It only causes hurt and pain
Look out to the horizon for the shore
Then uncertainty remains no more

Look into your soul and you will see
He knows everything that will be
Remain positive and look to the light
Soon you will know that things are alright

Believe

All you need is to believe
Amazing what you will achieve
Go for your desires without fear
What you wish for is very near

Now you know how to pray
Do not fear what to say
He waits for your first move
What you need is in that groove

You have it all inside your heart
Now it is time to make that start
His hand is extended out to you
You must make your dreams come true

Your reward will happen in a while
Walk forward with a smile
See yourself at the end
Fame and fortune will be your friend

I Lifted My Eyes

Surrounded by concrete and too many cars
I lifted my eyes and looked to the stars
Suddenly my world seemed so peaceful
I began to realize why I am so grateful

Life goes so quickly, so it seems
We forget to be still and watch moon beams
I thought about the feel of a gentle breeze
Stopping to laugh; having friends to tease

I thought about the first time that I saw snow
About the time that I held a doe
The scent of a rose with morning dew
Wishing my dreams would all come true

I remembered going on my first sleigh ride
The love of my life sitting by my side
I went digging for gold in abandoned caves
Adventure is what my heart craves

Watching a dolphin swim in the sea
So much pleasure, this brings to me
An eagle flying with so much grace
I soon realize that I love this place

An abundance of beauty at my fingertips
A big sigh soon escapes my lips
Everyone else can speed and scurry
I am enjoying life; not being in a hurry

Seeing sunshine even in the dark
Taking a walk in the park
Loving my Creator for what He sends
My appreciation of life never ends

Path without Fear

So many times in life we try to direct ourselves, thinking that we know which path to take.

We forget that humanly we may try to force our direction to go the way we want, instead of listening to Him.

Life is always uncertain, yet if we look at it without fear, it can be an exciting new adventure.

Walking a path without fear takes complete faith, knowing that He knows our future.

In our lives, we can grow accustomed to a daily routine, fearful of making changes in our lives.

We write on calendars, make our plans, as if in total control of everything and everyone else.

When things change, and things do not go the way we think they should, we may become fearful, or even look down upon ourselves.

It is difficult, humanly, to begin walking a new path, and go in a different direction.

Perhaps, when one realizes that when walking in complete faith, things turn out so much better.

It is then time to look at each new day differently, and without any fear at all.

Allowing Him to take our hand, we may find that what we thought we wanted wouldn't have worked out at all.

Take a path without fear, and see the sunrise, knowing now you will be led to a better opportunity in life, with enjoyment, wonder and excitement.

Jigsaw Puzzle

Sometimes our lives seem like a jigsaw puzzle. The pieces are scattered and the picture is unclear. We must start with the outer edges first; then we slowly progress, trying to find another piece to fit and connect to the edges. Often times, it seems frustrating, with the end appearing to be so far away. Yet, if we continue with patience, we will fit more and more pieces together, until finally the picture becomes clear and complete.

We all have a purpose or mission in life. As infants, we are content to coo, be held, fed and receive the simple basics given to us, which sustain our lives. As we gradually grow, we will assume more of the responsibilities, learning as we go along. We learn by trial and error, just was we try to fit the correct pieces into a puzzle.

We soon are taught that life gives us alternatives, choices and unavoidable incidents. Some seem sad or seemingly wrong, but along with the good things that happen, every bit of life is necessary to teach us the lessons we need to survive and carry out our purpose. At the time, we often feel overloaded, and cannot see or understand why we run into these problems. However, later on, when all of the puzzle pieces come together, we soon can make sense of why these things occurred. We also must be thankful that each and every part happened, as it contributes to the final connection of our purpose or mission.

In finality; just like putting puzzles together; the more we do, the easier these tasks become. We gain increased understanding of why everything happens in life, and that all of it serves a purpose in the big picture. We should look at the people and events that cross our paths as a new adventure or learning experience, as well as a tool meant to lead us further. When we see where we are now, we realize that if everything had not occurred as it did, we would not have been able to travel to our destination. All of a sudden, the picture we have created makes perfect sense, and we can smile at our final accomplishment.

United We Stand

It seems to me that life is grand
For with God, united we stand
The chain of love is getting strong
By His side, we can't do wrong

With each other, we continue to grow
Seeking His truth as we sow
We form a bond across the land
Each of us extending our hand

Our love for each other now is passed
Hatred and sorrow, outward is cast
A new heart and soul, we try to reach
Love and kindness is what we teach

Love of life is understood
Passing this on, as we should
Somehow we know that in a while
More and more will show that smile

The power of love will always win
God looks down and has a grin
Like hair that starts with one strand
Into fullness, united we stand

Seeing the Light

Right now I am seeing the light
It shines so beautifully bright
My path is finally clear
My Creator's intent is very near

Everything happens for a reason
I now am entering His season
I will listen very carefully
What is coming next, I will see

Even if some things happen badly
I will not live life sadly
My mission will carry me far
Now I realize where you are

I have so much more I must do
Special friends will help me too
Like listening to a peaceful sound
Around me now, His arms surround

Some of the places where I went
Where not of my own intent
Over the hurdle, He forced me to go
Truth and destiny, I will now know

Look Towards Tomorrow

Put away that sorrow
Look to tomorrow
It is a new beginning
See yourself winning

Some things you cannot change
Plans you will rearrange
Accept the life you are in
Rise up that chin

Do not make a commotion
Travel in a forward motion
Count your blessings now
Do not worry about how

For every new season
All happens for a reason
Instead of crying and whining
See the bright sun shining

Ideas will bring a new conception
You will go in a new direction
Ask the Creator up above
To continue surrounding you with love

For now, just do your best
He will handle all the rest
This anguish will not last
It is now part of your past

Escape from Negativity

When I am bombarded with negativity
I surround myself with nature's creativity
Animals show honesty in all they do
Their emotions never false, but always true

Erosions caused by people make me cry
Nature's untouched beauty makes me sigh
Giving life utmost respect
Never showing others any neglect

I find myself questioning way up high
Seeing world ugliness and wondering why
If all was created by total love
Why do people push and shove?

Choosing to look forward to each day
Wanting to end sadness is what I pray
Instead of seeing darkness in the night
I look forward to dawn's early light

Turning something bad into something good
Not easy to do, but try we should
From unhappiness I turn away
Go forth with peacefulness is what I say

When Life Gets Tough

When life gets tough, take the bull by the horns
At times it seems there are too many thorns
Life always has its ups and downs
But we must rid ourselves of those frowns

Life is how you see it, whether good or bad
Try very hard to turn sad to glad
When dark clouds are all you see
Turn them into rainbows and feel glee

When those heart strings feel that pull
Know that your glass is really half full
You may feel as though you have hit ground
Count your blessings, soon happiness is found

Give to others as they give to you
In the end love always pulls you through
As you listen to life's music, it only takes a while
There is bound to be something to make you smile

Take a few moments to stop and reflect
Everything created has cause and effect
Soon you will see that life is not so rough
Feel your strength and beauty when life gets tough

I B M

Listen now, I do not jest
Imagine, Believe, Manifest

Just Imagine in your mind
Soon that image you will find

If you Believe in what you need
Soon it will materialize indeed

Now prepare for the best
The vision will now Manifest

This is a positive belief I share
I use this right along with prayer

Soon this practice you will hone
God's plan for you will be shown

Close your eyes and see your goal
Positive thoughts enter your soul

Follow your heart as you must
Give it all of your deepest trust

Use patience and take your time
Dreams turn to reality sublime

Cheerful Heart

What you first say
Starts up your day
If you wear a big smile
It lasts a long while

Say something nice
Happiness you entice
Smile like you should
Make friends feel good

Life a positive staff
Make them all laugh
Try not to be tearful
It is better to be cheerful

You can help people cope
Give smiles and some hope
Show friends you care
Give love and a prayer

Hurt goes away fast
When a grin you make last
Being positive at the start
Will lead to a cheerful heart

Miracles

God works his miracles, just wait and see
If you believe hard enough, then it will be
When you stop and say a prayer
Know that He is always there

He listens to what you say
Then He sends you on your way
He protects you from the storm
He will always keep you warm

Nothing is too much for Him
Even if you have a whim
Start reaching for that star
For He knows who you are

His love is pure and true
He shows that He loves you
You will be very wise
If you pray and claim your prize

Anything is possible to those who believe
If you think it in your mind, you will conceive
Take away all doubt and fear
Know that miracles are near

Behold the Sunshine

This morning to darkness, I awoke
Later on, as if He spoke
"Look up; behold the bright sunshine"
"Know that all life is by my design"

I have to smile, because I know it is true
He guides me in everything that I do
The world may not always be a happy place
But it is important to keep a smile on my face

I try to take hurt and confusion in my stride
I know who is standing by my side
I quietly watch His creatures every day
They seem to teach me in their own way

After each season, I have found
I question why I ever frowned
A gift of life bestowed upon me
With each day passing, my heart is set free

As long as my Creator remains above
I will continue spreading my love
From every sunrise to each sunset
What is to come, will be the best yet

Crossroads of Life

I come to the fork in the road
Deciding where to drop off my load
Should I go left, or should I go right?
My decision is with you in my sight

I am grateful when I awake
My mission is always for love's sake
So nice to live life without any fear
A peaceful feeling as long as you remain near

The music that goes through my ears
Is so beautiful, it brings me to tears
Now I know you will not go away
For here in my heart you decided to stay

Our lives have so many ups and downs
But it does no good to wear those frowns
My decision has been made, where I will go
Crossroads of life without any woe

Into the Fold

Those who truly have hearts of gold
Will gather more friends into the fold
When around the bend darkness lurks
Remember you are rewarded for your works

Walk through the fire without any fear
Only goodness does the Creator hear
With wings of protection we shall go
Truth prevails and that we know

Together those alike will take a stand
Our purpose in life will be grand
For everything there is a reason
We look forward to the new season

We shall cast our doubts aside
As we travel on a glorious ride
Our goals may take some extra time
In the end it is worth the climb

Guiding Light

He has called me to His guiding light
Feelings inside of me seem so right
By keeping my heart and soul in tune
My destiny to be revealed some time soon

As humble as I may be
He still has called on me
The One who leads me from above
Is showing me how to spread His love

At one time I would rarely pray
Now through Him it happens every day
My life has purpose and a goal
As now He has entered into my soul

Truth revealed through different ways
Inside my heart is where it lays
Keeping a smile upon my face
While He leads me to that perfect place

I promise as long as I shall live
Through Him I will always give
Keeping love going day and night
Being led by His guiding light

Into the Light

Moving forward, traveling through a tunnel

Being gently and slowly drawn towards a white beam of light

Feelings of peacefulness; letting my body be led

No sadness, regrets, or feelings of things left undone

Embracing the unknown; knowing that beauty lies beyond

Awakening with joy, that life has given me another day

Appreciating the blessings I have

Not knowing how much longer life may exist

Taking one day at a time, and stopping to smell the roses

Being happy to have known and experienced love in many ways

To give more than I expect to receive

To accept life as it is, and make the most of it

To smile at every opportunity up until the last moment

Love of Life

To love life, I have found that you must embrace all of your experiences and accept the environment you are in any period of time. There are reasons that may not be understood, as to why the cards are dealt to us. The events that happen to us are not as important as how we deal with each situation as it arises, as well as the attitudes that we carry forward.

Each time that I wondered why a certain situation occurred in my life, I realized that I always learned something from it, enabling me to grow stronger for the next event. It is never easy to smile after adversity, but if your quest is to live for the next adventure, you will survive and carry on.

The unknown can be very exciting and filled with anticipation of what lies ahead in your future. To be able to see beauty at a slower pace, and enjoy your surroundings as often as possible, will make your journey more fulfilled with happier experiences. Smiling can make you feel healthier, and spreads a positive feeling to others around you. It is an action that is as contagious as any disease, but is more attainable from even a distance. It is just as simple to pass happiness around as sadness, but most people prefer to live as happy a life as possible. Happy people are much more fun to be around.

When you find that people enjoy your companionship, you must realize that your love of life is the cause. Loving life is something that will extend your longevity, and will carry you through until your journey is over. When I wake up in the morning, I ask myself how I feel. If I do not feel happy, I write the reasons for my sadness down on paper, then attempt to find a quick resolve. In a short matter of time my love of life returns along with my smile and happy heart.

Linda's Quotes

"Life is only limited to the depth of your imagination"

"Every day is a 'new' day, full of opportunities, adventure and a chance to make your dreams come true."

"Never stop at dreaming your dream. See it becoming reality. Imagine, believe, manifest."

"Wake up with sunshine in your heart, a smile upon your face, and your day will be beautiful and full of peacefulness."

"Dwell not on negativity in our world; instead awake with gratitude and a sense of adventure. Seize the day."

All quotes are original and are written by Linda Andrusko

Meet the Author

Linda Andrusko was born in Southern California, but later migrated to Minnesota, and finally moved with her husband to Sequim, Washington.

She has two grown twin sons, one grandson of her own, and shares two grandchildren with her husband.

Her love of writing began with her father telling her that she should write, a few years before he passed away. Because she was not totally confident in her abilities, she waited until she read Yanni's book, "Yanni in Words", which gave her the courage to try writing her first home made book. The response from many who received a free copy of her book was so uplifting, that she has decided to write from her heart, whenever the muse allows her to do so.

Her favorite writings are 'God' inspired, and meant to uplift others, and make them smile. She also likes to write about nature, wildlife, music, love, and a little bit of humor or whimsy.

Her philosophy and quote in life is: "Every day is a 'new' day, full of opportunities, adventure and a chance to make your dreams come true."

Made in the USA
Charleston, SC
23 October 2012